The Spoken Body

Yolanda Nieves

Plain View Press
P. O. 42255
Austin, TX 78704

plainviewpress.net
sb@plainviewpress.net
512-441-2452

Copyright Yolanda Nieves 2009. All rights reserved.
ISBN: 978-1-935514-45-9
Library of Congress Number: 2010920360

Cover art by Hellen Coleman
Cover design by Susan Bright

Acknowledgments

Some of these poems have been previously published in *Coloring Book: An Eclectic Anthology of Fiction and Poetry* by *Multicultural Writers*, *The Journal of Ordinary Thought*, *The Teacher's Voice*, and *Dialogo:* Center for Latino Research at DePaul University, Chicago.

Also by Yolanda Nieves:

Poetry
Dove Over Clouds

Plays
Brown Girls Singing (Co-authored with Sandra Posadas)
The Brown Girls' Chronicles: Puerto Rican Women and Resilience

For the women we really are.

Contents: The Spoken Body

Body Of Interpretations

The Invention Of Myself	9
When I Write	11
Photos In the Box	13
Her Only Poem	14
Longing	15
Tomasa Otero Enters My Dream	17
Stoned	19
Neglect	21
Magazine Picture	23
Mujer de Guatemala In the Years Of the War	24
Warning In Black and Blue	26
Falsely Named	27

Body Of a Woman

Body Of a Woman	31
A Chance Meeting With an Old Lover	33
Obsession	35
How a Poet Loves Another Poet	37
Fantasy	39
Crow's Feet	40
Unsolicited Kiss	42
Slow Boat	43
Varicose Veins	44
The Obvious Truth When Love Is Gone	46

Body Of Institutions

In Response To the Question What Inspired You To Start Writing	51
Urban Issues In Education	52
Student Teaching	56
Teaching Poetry	57
Lunch Time	59
The Lesson	60
Homework	62
High School Hallway	63
The Shape Of a Story	65

Second Thoughts On the Teaching Profession	67
Last Day	69
Terrorists Of the New Decade Or Who Showed Up In Homeroom Today	71
The First Puerto Rican Librarian	74

Body Of Displacement

Neighborhood Boys	79
Gentrification	81
Displacement	82
Going Home	84
It Used To Be	87
On the Northwest Corner Of the 3200 Block Of West Thomas Street, Chicago	90
Lucky Find	93
Roses	95
Early Morning Ritual	96

Body Of Odd Thoughts

Waiting	101
An Anaphora About Preferences	102
Innocence	104
Answered Prayer	105
Ode To Directions	106
Would You Still Invite Frida Khalo To Dinner?	109
All About Bull	111

About the Author 115

Body Of Interpretations

The Invention Of Myself

I have increased my chances
of living

since I have identified
myself

as alive
truly human

based on the notion of
spirituality

not on the mechanics of
biology

I am a pattern, a fabric
woven together
like the roots of a baobab tree
netted into the earth.

This is a new experiment
a woman acknowledging herself

speaking in her own voice
embracing her own softened

body

knowing

continued…

the physical distance
between
heart and mind
is
a new agreement

a complete picture appears.

When I Write

> *Think carefully of the history*
> *that in love united us.*
> *Take good care of the present*
> *and don't disturb my voice.*
>   Julia de Burgos
>   "The First Tears"

A hand quivers while
penning a story

in loops
in unfamiliar scrawls

it is my hand
splitting old thoughts
enclosed by the shell
of the years.

I think of love,
my hand writes of sorrow.

I think of today,
the fingers insist I write
of yesterday.

Words start in English
and end in Spanish.

Lost in the forest of
my own penmanship
I dig to find some sweet
marrow in this bone of
memory I chew.

continued…

Bodies with wings, faces of dust,
silent fog,
float across the pages
then the lips of a shadow
curls a breath in my ear—
it is all blown into the night.

When I sleep
these ghosts suspend
my body over the
water of time.

I become Julia in the river
of Loiza
in a place known only to us
in the liquid of my dreams.

We flow to the place
where my mother washed clothes
as a young girl
where my father chased his brother
into a brook
and my grandmother gathered water.

While I sleep these moons of memory
rise
setting in the muscles of my fingers

my hands are theirs
the pen keeps moving.

Photos In the Box

Chicago's Division Street hollow of cars
looks quiet in black and white
except for my smile
smoky in the frost of that
winter's day.

In another photo
blanketed in hospital cotton
my mother holds me;
she stares at my face
what makes her look
so sad?

Then there is this one—
my body small
round behind a birthday cake
framed by faces
I don't know anymore
tiny stones floating into the ocean
disappearing into time.

My memory is like rain
for many days it doesn't come
then floods me all at once.

Her Only Poem

Not being able to return
to see her dying mother
erased a piece of her faith
in the world.

My mother wept under
an unbearable red sky
one evening

on a piece of pallid butcher paper
she wrote her first poem
with the same hands

she peeled bananas
fried meat, scrubbed floors, and
untangled knots from my hair.

I've lost the paper—

whatever she wrote must
have been beautiful.

She wrote her grief
opening the folds of
her sadness
on paper

braver than
I ever could be.

Longing

This night is too heavy
to bear alone

my mother's voice
like a river
bends in strange places.

I cling to her skirt
then walk with her—

she calls to her mother
who is gone
she can't see the face anymore.

From the corner of my eye
a wind puffs a curtain

        ¿Que buscas hija?
        ¿Buscas la vida?
        La vida se va volando.

I watch her eyes travel
into empty rooms
her fingers caress a small

cross of gold hanging
around her neck
a gift from her mother.

Outside a radio rattles in Spanish
music floats from a neighbor's kitchen.

I have slipped with her into
a space of remembering;

continued…

my grandmother wipes her hands on
her housecoat of flowers
the soft skating

of garlic and cilantro
sliding in hot olive oil.

My damp forehead wrinkles in wonder—
I am afraid
the beauty of the world
could be buried stones

under my memory.

The old woman who sat on the porch
laughing with neighbors has vanished.

Did she ever think of other ways
to spend her life?
Now my mother sits in the hours

longing to hear the voice
of her mother cooing

> *¿Que buscas hija?*
> *¿Buscas la vida?*
> *La vida se va volando.*

Tomasa Otero Enters My Dream

It is her hand I feel in mine
rough fingers like the coastal
stones of Manati
the Atlantic salt water moisture
settling in her palms
cleanses mine.

Her neighbors
long gone or dead
poke their heads from windows
their bodies are cracks of light
in doorways
faces outlined by darkness
they wave their arms
then dissipate—

> *Can our testimony*
> *be heard? Our innocence affirmed?*

Sugar cane stains
the blood of her fathers
melted on flesh
it is my brown identity

that has not been swallowed by
the mouth of this city, this country
no one sees me
I am invisible—
> *Will there, can there*
> *be another way of living?*

continued…

Transplanted
a forced migration
after forced sterilization
made her hold my hand hard

the first granddaughter
born outside the island
will be shaped to remember
an old world, old ways;

cilantro sprouts grow
in windowsill boxes
beans give a shy salutation
in a neighbor's yard
the earth is everything

she tells me this every night.

Now mangoes and breadfruit
need visas, they arrive in boxes
folded banana leaves
colonized in plastic wrappers
inspected by soldiers
are liberated by her hands.

This language she poured on the
rocks of my life
are sacred stories.

I am liberated by her life.

        I am her place of forgiving.

Stoned

Standing in the empty lot
next to the liquor store
I squeeze
in the palm of my hand
a rough stone
while I wait for my father.

The eye of the stone
stares back at me
I consider
I may have lost something
I needed but never had.

I pretend to float
in the pool of the open sky
gliding to some kind of place
not sure yet
of what to think
of a childhood buried
under a drunken father's
vomit.

He leans on my shoulder
to keep from falling, as I
help him balance himself back
home my mother sees him,
and turns away.

She locks all the windows
we live breathless.

continued…

From above I see
I am always alone
never unafraid
under the covers
behind a locked door
beneath the horizon
squeezing the stone

while my father takes another drink.

Neglect

There is a river that takes us
beyond loneliness
our parents left us there
we will be together
forever
little sister
in that desolate place.

Our arms are stretched water
our eyes anchors
we are each other's harbor.

In those summers of rain
when we were left alone
our mother working
our father nowhere to be found

staring out the same window
the cat of night crept in
to silence the scream
of our eyes.

What did we know about sin?
Theirs? Ours?
Where were our stars?

With one key between the
two of us
we preferred our bedroom
door closed
our days connected by loneliness.

continued…

The small tragedy of

hours surrounding us
hunger abiding in us

we know we lived this together
little sister
no need to speak of it.

Magazine Picture

The infant at her breast
no longer cries
hunger has made it old
her breast is shriveled
with clouds absent from
the sky's wide pain,
lack of water seems
to be a worry.

I glance at her eyes.
Does she wish for a blanket
a tin of beans,
sleep?

Living on the brink of nowhere
life is a shadow—
I take a quick
second look—

the dust
around her, sheath
under her feet—
those ashes surrounding her
mean something.

Rotting nearby is a
withered hibiscus plant.

I think of a ripe melon
then of despair
that will split open
to drip down her side—

I quickly turn the page.

Mujer de Guatemala In the Years Of the War

*My experience is as a witness to the genocide which occurred in Guatemala.
I have learned that there is no such thing as a just war. No war is just.*
                         Rigoberta Menchu
                         Hague Appeal for Peace
                         Opening Ceremonies 1999

You are a Mayan parable
a lesson with broken arms and legs;
the consciousness of a country
braided tightly around your head.
Sky, sun, earth
they leave a list of scars
healed by the birth of the coffee beans you sow.

The popping of distant gunfire keeps you awake.
You sleep with your eyes open waiting to make
a treaty with the morning. You are guarded by
the faces of your brethren that smile in the fog.
You wave. They are your namesake, the disappeared.
Herbs and flowers honor them on your alter by the stove.

Suddenly the night is made red and orange by your sons
hung like burning torches swinging upside down
from your papaya tree.

You dream you are inside a truck, wrists tied behind
your back. Questions. Blood. More questions.
Your Quiche tongue waves like a shredded red flag
tied to the snout of a machine gun. Thighs are opened
like the throat of a singing bird. Many men enter you
digging deep enough to break a well of blood.

Arms unfurl your body into a crowded ditch.
Rain moistened your lips. Death glanced your way.

A thirsty chick squats by the aches of your torched home.
You curl the old rosary blessed by *el padresito* in your palm.
The bananas tied to the hinge of your door are ripened black
good only for flies and maggots.

Your daughters scattered like seeds in the nearby mountains
are the little rivers in your eyes.
The flesh of your men seeped in mud, pecked by hungry birds,
feed the foliage.

The sound of silence is speckled with the wailing of
women by the graves.

There are quiet things left; the soft breathing of the trees,
the smoky fingers that rise from a morning fire,
church bells clang in the distance and a long
horizon of stories rolled into a ball
translated into a whisper from your scream.

Warning In Black and Blue

Fist. Bruise. Blood. Tears.
A house of cruel and angry winds.
She may stay ten years more.
He won't change, but she hopes—

that is her prison.

Falsely Named

Paloma, Ying, or *Fatima*
preferred, please.

Not this name
that tumbles head first
from my mouth into

the soft weeping of
lonely flower draped
across a bed.

My body is wrong for it—
eyes, nose, mouth,
disproportionate in spirit
incompatible in character.

We disappear so quickly.
Why should our names
be the circumference
that circles our whole lives?

I want my name to be
an entire continent of skies
with sunshine
          Nalaya

an olive tree or
an afternoon by the ocean
with a pearl between my toes
          Màirèad

a sweet autumn apple or
a bird with wide wings

continued…

that flies in the rain
nobly
                Nabila

not the broken heart
of a Spanish ballroom
dancer.

Body Of a Woman

Body Of a Woman

Loving you is what I do best
in English
        desire

in Spanish
        amor

midnight and noon
with tequila or champagne

in the back seat of cars
in the empty storeroom against
buckets and brooms

giddy, dizzy
delinquent, greedy.

Let's reap the early flame
of passion
hidden in the margins

unbraiding the knot of propriety
I grow lovely in the dark
in the velvet of passion
        palabras de pasión.

Unraveling myself
in the leisure of your flesh
curling inward and outward
making good use of naked time

running my hand
against the sweat-rivers of your back
you lick my wrists and fingers

continued…

together we are wine
red
thick
rich.

I become drenched bread
the cleavage of a ripe peach
after being bitten

your tongue a wisp of breath
on my lips.

A Chance Meeting With an Old Lover

From afar your gaze brushes my cheeks pink
your light eyes travel into my dark ones

you have a face I remember;

your laughter, then silence
the way you took your coffee
or ran you palms along the silk of my thighs
is a dead tree in a forest of memory.

Did we hold hands while sleeping?
Exchange stories of a childhood woe?
How was it with us so long ago?
How did we say goodbye? Who said it first?

This tight braid of a memory
needs to be undone—
my eyes comb your body.

I turn myself around inside
an odd old ache swells
I become an afterbirth
stretched
red—
the sudden wind of a memory
paralyzes me.

Somewhere a planet explodes
a telephone rings
I know nothing except to ask

what was this thing you
etched on my heart?

continued…

This thing is too
big to remember,
to heavy to carry
and I don't want to.

Obsession

Neruda's memory
of his lover's white breasts
makes me think of my own;

two exposed hearts facing the moon
soft as ripe mango meat
waiting to be cupped by
a pulsing hand

cascading mother of pearls
draped against my chest
they have their own
perfect strength
two civilizations rising from
the landscape of flesh

passionate witnesses to time
like the murmur of doves
content to swell behind
the shadow of leaves
they rest

citizens of a private republic

that place between them
is a smooth valley of milk

I lay my hand
where I want to tremble
a place lovers desire
with no shield or shroud
it is a land unclaimed

continued…

it is there I want to love you
junto a mi,
next to me
tonight.

How a Poet Loves Another Poet

The attraction is purely spiritual
at first—

on a bicycle, taxi
car, bus
I travel miles to
behold you
in the dim light
of an greasy bar.

Mouthing words
to a poem you've written
while you stand behind
a microphone
reminding the world to open its arms

my ears are nets
I lower them to catch what spills
out of your mouth.

In the corner the jukebox
stops long enough
so I can hear my favorite
last line.

Later our knees touching under the table
faces close
one breath sustains me
then a wish
      make me a poem, take me home with you.

continued...

You grasp my fingers
squeezing away my questions like water from hair
our hands know how to love

books
paper
pencils
each other.

Fantasy

Rising and falling
like the sway of the ocean
the roundness of my hips
follow me—

they are the force of desire
mirrors of my name
symmetrical moons
enormous
two hills
round

plunging into a valley
a monument to womanhood
feminine fruit of the body
papaya, guava,
candied sweets.

Your eyes aquatic
become a tide splashing
behind me
your fingers are talons
they grasp from behind

the curves of ripe peaches
gentle slopes dimpled in your hands
honey combs dripping sweetness
then settling in the middle of
your dream.

My wave crashes into the flame
then another
silencing your moan.

Crow's Feet

It is the hour when the sun
nudges the truth forward
what quietly hovered over my shoulder
in the mirror yells out: OLD!

I recoil—

a new line has arrived
in a face already crowded
with tiny crevices
reminders of an anxious youth
now more obvious
as the days fold forward.

Pondering my reflection
I see more than I want;

how strange and sudden
a sleepless night shrouds
the brightness of the eyes

little trails determined
to travel farther than they should go like the
tips of roots that spring mysteriously
in aging soil.

I avoid the bright room
pull myself inside.

To be young again

one would have to shed stories
erase details of little agonies
debate new causes
deny pledges of affection, remember
prayers answered and unanswered;

I would need to forget how I cried when
I left the scared cat behind
in the old house

my joy in finding her again
under my mother's folded sheets
the grooves in my face beckoning
familiarity.

Embossed on the folds of my flesh
are my many lives
reflecting the world I've
come to know so well.

I am
opaque
comfortable
transparent
no longer have reasons
to run
or hide.

Curling toward the neck
a new expedition.
The future is carved
in permanent lines.

Unsolicited Kiss

That moment
between inhalation and suspiration

explodes

our lips threaded together
welded between space
and time

my mouth becomes the eye of a hurricane—

I reside in the sun and the moon
at the same time

Jumping upward
falling downward I
press myself completely against a wall

where quarters and octaves
are played by the orchestra of a mighty wind
swallowed by a darling bird of a tongue

a trickle of water falls from my eye
I laugh and cry
break the shell of myself open

this fever is never enough.

Slow Boat

The sailing of my body
has slowed to a hum

this nape of my neck
the place where beautiful boys
used to nuzzled their lips
spills over in little accordion folds;

a thin parchment of skin
that I can pull with two fingers
is less liquid than before—

torso rounded permanently
with the sitting of years
its memoirs are children that
kicked the womb pink

months of enormous stretching
and birthing watered the muscles.

I pause

over my body
blue ripple of veins
web my legs in odd places

under breasts so tired
they curl downward
resting on a flaccid belly.

I must travel in this ship—
my compass, my sails
my body.

Varicose Veins

When all I wanted was
beauty
forever
the fingers of time
decided to draw
blue lines on my legs.

Puffy curls in luminous strands
of blue
some the blush of
a violet petal
rising to the most
northern border
of my skin
so deliberate
I count them—

ten.

I found them the day I
dug for a safety pin,
panty hose,
a lacey pink bra
in an old drawer.

Stretching hose over my
rippled thighs

ten.

There are true-sad tales of women,
a manifestation of age
my eyes navigate the routes—

ten new routes.

I stare at the
pulsing river sculptures
highways that churn the flesh
remaining imbedded
like caterpillars
some finger-shaped
others broken
scattered webs

ribbons wrapped
around my thighs
surrounded, cuffed
I am a river, a road, a map.

Unwanted roots
like weeds buried
in my flesh

my body covered in
fine lines.

The Obvious Truth When Love Is Gone

Your desire knocks with castanets
and guitars at my door
behind the curtain
my eyes are soft summer plums
I don't want to look.

Your arms explode
with purple callas
my favorite;

your offering is a smooth
calculation baiting
my weakness
we are ravenous for the fire
in our hips.

Indecisive
suspicious of betrayal
again
my breath fogs the glass.

It is your eyes that frighten me most
more than anything
it is their passion that lingers
like fingers
touching all of me.

Lust, that bitter milk of humankind
leaves nothing but bones
battered, dry
too weak to resurrect.

True,
I adored your hands
that clutched my thighs
how you reached into that space
I gave freely
sweetly.

Suddenly—
a sob
too friendly to be a stranger
escapes my throat.

The doorbell tires of ringing
no explanations needed.

Body Of Institutions

In Response To the Question What Inspired You To Start Writing

When the librarian in grammar school
couldn't find stories or poems
with names like

Feliciano,
Otero,
Rodriquez, or
Santiago,

and I was sternly informed
that the only good poets
were the classical poets born in Europe,

and I got sent to the
principal's office for
calling the teacher a liar

when she told the class
there were no smart
or important
Puerto Ricans
in history.

Urban Issues In Education

for anyone who has survived Chicago's public school system

Too many students
not enough books
a teacher is absent amd
the substitute just doesn't like
the looks
of things—
leaves before lunch;

metal detectors
lunch room inspectors
mice snuggle in the food
the principal is not in the mood
to deal with leaky roofs
broken windows
and the fight
in the bathroom
during lunch;

while

fists keep flying in the hallway
cracked teeth on the floor
parents yelling in the main office
another student is thrown
out the door
don't come back
expelled for good
the rest of you
in detention
there will be no redemption
mis-educated for good,

no good
we are so
misunderstood

after lunch

broken computers
knife under a desk
stay for attendance
leave before the test
that will indicate
your lack
of academic progress
sit in the back
because you lack
the social skills
that will help heal
the community's ills

Never mind
they don't know
you have no heat
frig is empty and
there's nothing to eat
at home
where the landlord roams
trying to get
your family evicted
while you get convicted
out in the street

in the courts
they debate

continued…

legislation
against segregation;
Blacks on one side
Mexicans on the other
Puerto Ricans in the middle
while some White kids
don't even bother
to come
to school

protected at home
waiting by the phone
home schooled by their mothers
until the magnet school calls
for the spot
in the halls
of academia
Has there been any progress?
not at all,
not for all.

Pot in the pocket
sell it for your mother's rent
guns in the school yard
come through the hole
in the fence
teacher thinks most of the kids
are retards, gangbangers, and
dense

while
art is cancelled and
contamination ruins the pool
math class is in the hallway
no one is fooled

that

politicians stand fascinated by
size of their paychecks
as equal opportunity
is all whittled away
what the heck?
Students are just flecks
of dust in their eyes
pains in their necks
just get lost
the systems a wreck:

while

they kill legislation
that can bring reformation
this lack of quality
symbolizes equality
is dead—
instead
children are deemed
it seems
too costly for society
no one seems to be sorry;

let's confess
schooling is a mess
there hasn't been any progress
at all

there hasn't been any
progress for all.

Student Teaching

Walking by classrooms disinfectant rising from
waxed floors, the hallway is silent
the last moment of summer is tucked away;

I open the day with hope—
they will arrive soon
with backpacks like folded wings,
little asterisks of eyes.

Some bring the steam
of grass and picnics on their skin
other shoulders bend, resigned to
a sad September.

I wonder about the

mist in the eyes
of the children
Soon the sky will be hidden
behind books
pencil sharpeners
long lunch lines.
Backs will arch reluctantly
into their papers—
a cold breath descends on us;
the urgent vigor of life
turns into whispering,
smothered laughter
presses to close lips.

Teaching Poetry

I read a poem a poet built
out of a rare stone of a moment.
This time my subject is a man
with the feet of a prophet, his words
thick with the flavor
of honey on bread.

My plan dangles from
the edge of a windowsill,
I swear to myself
this is the poem-the one they will carry
forever—
a lucky coin in their pocket.

Even as they sit in a circle
sniffling, sculpting whispers,
eyes are darts on the bulls eye
of the clock
counting the thousands of
seconds until dismissal time.
Others note the dust
on the teacher's desk.

I throw fire into the snow
of their eyes,
I imagine them cheering
from the sidelines,
applauding the words I explain—
a single road split into two halves
we live among choices
we belong to each other.
Learn this, please.

continued…

I grow suddenly lonely.
No one is listening.
The way I travel is always
looking backward
talking to the living, thinking of
the dead.

Is anyone following me?

Lunch Time

You know only that
in a minute the bell
will ring;
nothing will resemble
order.

Their eyes travel to
the clock on the wall
the silver needle
points to relief.

Lunch tickets are maps
they lead to a safe passageway
the quick meal is shade from the press
of a difficult morning.

The food will keep them
from drifting away;
for you a moment
of quiet

where you try to
remember the circle
of your passion for learning,
but where did you last
placed your keys?

You can't explain
how you walked your way
into this old profession.
Teachers often hold
a sandwich between their fingers
not tasting a thing.

The Lesson

A whistle at recess
cuts their laughter in half

these children have been birds so long
they forgot about their legs.

They know the story of school—
straight rows
copying words from the board
a pin is supposed to drop
somewhere soon
We should all hear
this sad sound.

Letters are looped into
smiles
two dots and an
upside down parenthesis
in the q's
just for fun.

In another classroom
a wrong answer can mean
an earthquake, hot lava,
a trip to the principal's office.

Turning pages has become
more important than

daydreaming
spitting out a third floor window
making a paper ball for recess
from gum wrappers
doodling pictures of dogs
that look like flowers upside down
or yelling out loud

what is true is

they have begun to
understand how
clouds can shrink
into tiny particles
in jars.

Homework

Evenings teachers and students travel separately
into different lives;
mornings I turn around in myself struggling
carry hope around my neck.

I collect homework
from an unruly flock of hands
I know the truth—

these papers are tea leaves where
the secret of their lives leaves a trail—
copied lines are stained with grease
someone's anger leaves a dry tear of
smeared of ink,

in a pocket a sad poem becomes a baseball
sharing space with a half-eaten lollipop,
a marble, dice, and a crumpled
forgotten dollar bill washed
a dozen times.

A few invent intrigue on how their math disappeared;
others wave homework like white
flags on a battlefield
they resist living inside failure

some bring nothing except a
dream to conquer
the sky, wind, and sea
without books

they believe the world waits for them
after school.
You grow wise with their excuses.

High School Hallway

The hallway has a circular plot
raw flesh exposed to viral violence
as I move from
classroom to classroom
the voices of adolescents
parched dry under florescent lights
gather by lockers
to inhabit gossip
scorning the history of the day

their fingers roll
imaginary cigarettes
that will be lit later;
I am bound to their
ripples and splashes of anger—
the hallway sweats with
tension stretched tight
in their faces

eyes, some bloodshot,
avoid me—
they carve me into a wall
I hold my books
hard against my chest
the way a soldier
does a bayonet.

In this place we travel separately. I am
a suspension bridge between
a direction and a void. This truth
settles on my forehead as

continued…

we do a careful dance
around one another
half of us are shrinking at our desks
the other stretch toward the window longing to
be released.

The Shape Of a Story

I say
a story is not wrapped the way
a candy bar is, nicely folded.

They stare in silence,
it bothers me
the sweaty smell of the classroom.

I explain
a story can take the shape
of what's under a shoe
the odd button in a drawer
the love note folded
into a paper airplane
all this you can claim
as your own,
I say.

Silence.

Someone's fingers snap
I get it—

the dead staring eye
of someone you knew
blood on the sidewalk
the barrel of a gun
the stink of spilt wine
a used condom in the elevator

continued…

an empty refrigerator
dog fight and dog flesh
bleeding in the basement
a hundred bucks gambled
to pass the time
the landlord
yelling
pay your rent!
"That's what I can write about, teacher!"

I sit smaller in my chair.
Layers have been peeled
off my expectations.

Perhaps it is not so important
to make too much of perfection.

Whose voices should be heard?
In this part of the city
reality is piled high

I feel the fatigue of a long day
coming on.

Second Thoughts On the Teaching Profession

The years of lessons
have taught me to see
how little I have traveled.

I go back to places
outlining the faces
I have filled
with the shape of words
with bold strokes of knowledge.

Trembling I pause.

My thoughts of civility
carry me forward
sometimes their empty charity
stuns me.

I imagine the children
gathering armfuls of stars
before they reached the earth

they should be lost in the dazzle of red—
apples, roses, sunsets.

I try to follow

but inside the classroom walls
my lessons grow thick
with weight—
I bore myself.

continued…

Sometimes hands rise and wave
their answers are paper airplanes
that can split the earth
when they fall.

Other days my
questions are wadded into
paper fists and toss away.

I realize we all need to fling something
out the window sometimes.

Last Day

There—
in the desk
dusty and sticky
a crumpled paper
with two breasts
drawn round in ink
a matchbook
a pencil broken
on purpose

in the deepest corner
forgotten house keys
gum stuck on the edge
of the desk
sharp enough to cut
my finger

an old test
with a note to a mother
crushed into a paper pancake.

I don't know how
the year grew suddenly short
I forgot to notice
the hours fleeing south
another season of students
come and gone.

A classroom door is slammed
one last time
then all alone with
erasers smothered in chalk dust,
the last of the paper clips
a caterpillar strung together.

continued…

Summer! Vacation!
All the things I know
leave
my heart split in two
half of me licking my wounds
the other
taking a breath.

Terrorists Of the New Decade Or Who Showed Up In Homeroom Today?

> *American youth have become public enemy No. 1 on which to pin society's woes, while taxpayers and government leaders avoid the real issues of shifting economic and cultural realities.*
> —Henry A Giroux

The truth is they are here:

Hip hopper
avante guard loving
heavy-metal guitar smashing,
Goth frightening
reggae and reaggeton rapping
folk and country, grunger
flash back '70's disco dresser

an active refusal to socialize to dominant values.

Anarchist. Marxist-socialist
Pan-africanist
orthodox, unorthodox
flag-waver
gun-toting, hero-worshipping
Catholic and Protestant
sun worshipping
Wiccan, environmentalist
Che t-shirt wearer

all in your face.

continued…

Refugee, immigrant
homeless, documented, undocumented
Buddhist, Taoist,
Hindi, Moslem
atheist, agnostic
mute, blind
autistic, dyslexic
EMH, ADH
pro-war, anti-war
ex-leftist child guerrilla
majority minorities

a condition of our democracy.

Boy-George impersonator
Cher wanna be
transgendered, bisexual
homosexual alternative lifestyle
bar hopper
tattooed body modifier
independent news blogger

they will not disappear.

Alcoholic, recovering addict
bipolar, depressed
just released from the psych ward
patient
artist, con-artist, drug-dealer
thief, gambler
foster child, runaway
left-handed, right handed
bastard and prostitute

neutrality is annihilation.

Chess freaks
sci-fi delusional
parentless single parents
police brutalized
elote sellers

tax evading taxpayers
future voters of America

grass rooted and homegrown
oppositional, anti-procedural
gifted and illiterate

this public school homeroom is a
national convention convened—

free thinking is a serious possibility.

The First Puerto Rican Librarian

Talking to you I think about her—

Pura Belprè

while sewing lace on dresses with her fingers
she was remembering stories with her heart.

pura means pure—

The winds of migration
blew her from Puerto Rico
to New York
hanging from a thread of

pure fate

she didn't return home
stayed in New York
after her sister's wedding.

In the boroughs
her story-hungry kinfolk
believed books ignored them
with no one to whisper of

the weeping island, heaps of cane,
rain, and family left behind;
the memories were

pure pieces

of heartbreak.

Pura Belprè

all arms, feet, and heart
collecting traditions, our oral histories,
thawing the ice that froze our tongues
she gave us back the blaze of our past

our stories have citizenship in books.

Body Of Displacement

Neighborhood Boys

Grayer skies now—
an old woman with no garden
weeps for her dead cat
flattened in the alley.

Boys ditch school
their anger a tight ball of wire
revolving against a sharp city
they shiver
backs against the wall.

They used to trade marbles
for baseball cards
play hide n' seek
jump fences
curl in the space
between garages

stoop behind garbage cans
streaks of grim
striped across their faces.

They ran after
the ice cream truck
kicked the can
while playing tag.

The woman is inside now
clutching her hands
in a darkened room
peeping behind the curtain

continued…

she wonders
how they grew up
to sit in cars
trade guns
still angry
shivering
backs against
the wall.

Gentrification

For my neighbors who have been displaced from Humboldt Park

There are less and less
children

playing on the block
and

more and more
dogs

sniffing
the empty lots

the city smells
rotten.

Displacement

City of shrinking shoulders
Chicago
can no longer fill
in the width of its
blue collar shirt

in the dying quiet
old Chi-town has
swept its residents
elsewhere
outside city limits.

Wanting what we had
suburban dwellers
flood the neighborhoods
like a stream of headlights
accelerating the ousting
of people, we are the
eyes of a deer staring
into oncoming traffic.

Armed with parking zone stickers they
anonymously report neighbors' rusty cars
for coveted curb space
in front of fine masonry houses
that bully the humble bungalow.

On my block
another neighbor leaves
scrapped away from all she has known—

when the rich cannot live
with the poor
the city shrinks

hardly anyone is left
to call out my name
admire daffodils
that grow on my lawn. No one
sits on my front porch
to gather the day's news

this sadness swells in my throat

the town we thought
so strong
without its people
is a thin piece of paper
blown by the wind.

The breathless skyline now scrawls
KEEP OUT!

What I loved best—the
scent of neighborhood kitchens
childrens' voices like timbres and bells
will be packed in boxes
all moved out.

Going Home

      I.

I am drenched with longing
the way a mango ripens
then waits for a gentle hand
on the low swinging branch
of an old tree

needing to be caught
before falling—

I am its flesh
splitting
ripe, sweet
on the ground
where everything
first began

my skin smells like nectar again

I blow a kiss to remembering.

      II.

Tribe of old rose bushes
growing by the gate
planted by my mother
most are withered
none bloom with rose buds.

I bend to smell the only bud I see,
a swarm of wasps surround me.

I climb sloping stairs
gray paint
ruffled like old feathers
cracks under my feet
it seemed I lived forever
in this old house
I've been gone too long.

III.

Missing her
my mothher—
I dreamed she called
in the middle of the night
the message muffled
by the song of a lone cricket
softly crying
wing caught on a rose bush thorn

between waking and waiting
my senses are fractured
this memory weaves then unweaves
the stories I was told

until everything becomes true
this is the fruit of my remembering;

old pictures on the dresser of her room
this tide of memory floods me
like the thunder of a wave, I am water
spilling everywhere.

IV.

Moving backward in time
apparitions want to hold my hand
rotting fruit in the kitchen must be thrown out
this gray house
these dry roses
there is grief I have yet to experience.

Dust rises up from the
edges of the wall.

There is a stirring in this well of memory
I stretch to
grasp whatever is left
careful not to fall.

V.

Walking backward to move forward
the destination is the same
the direction is different
memories are shaped like seeds
some grow perplexed
some shine more that the silver
dollar I found under
my mother's old mattress.

There are letters in the mailbox
I still have to read.

It should not be so difficult
to open the windows.

It Used To Be

It used to be
that as you walked down Division Street
the windows would wave you in
with Hector Lavoe, Willie Colon, and Celia Cruz
salsa and mambo rhythms—

everyone was dancing all the time
from the *pan con café* breakfast
to the red beans and rice dinner.

Everyone carried baskets of *buenos dias*
I could feel the *sofrito*, the blended herbs of garlic
and cilantro under my skin, taste it, too.

It used to be
the lights of the Teatro San Juan
would blink, "Come in! Come in!"
You could see Cantinflas movies from Mexico,
bullfight updates from Spain, and Tom and Jerry
cartoons in Spanish. That language was our boat
we'd sail above the
No Puerto Rican's Wanted Here signs
in the mean parts of the city.

Vanilla and orange sherbet pops were
only fifteen cents. The popcorn was
always rich, creamy, hot. Everyone was your cousin,
you'd share everything.

It used to be
whoever saw you knew you.
They'd yell, "*Hola Comai*," and "*Hola Compai*," and
"*Como te va hoy?*"

continued…

        "Mira la negrita, que grande esta,"
and someone would pinch my cheeks until it hurt.

You could cross the street to your grandmother's house and
hear audio-novelas while she cooked pork chops and fried plantains.
Neighbors would stop by for a couple of potatoes,
a can of chick peas,
and a cup of coffee.

You'd get your groceries on credit from Fuentes' Bodega. Lollipops
were only a penny, and he'd tell your mother if you were hanging
around with the wrong crowd.

After school, I'd sit behind the counter of my uncle's store—
Borinquen Record Shop and Botanica, where for ten cents you
could buy a candle to light to *La Senora de la mas Altisima* and
Santa Barbara-they'd make your woes disappear.

It used to be
you felt right at home on Division Street,
you wouldn't get lost in your own neighborhood
pedacito de patria.

The people have almost all disappeared. Time, like a butter knife,
has spread us away from each other. Sometimes I dream that I
hear my grandmother laugh loosely and loud
or she is humming under her breath.
I bite my tongue between my teeth
it hurts to remember so much. I want to press
this dream to my lips.

No one would stare at you as if your were a crack in the wall
of a new house, as if you didn't belong. Now I watch
my neighbors from the corner of my eye with an unnatural
suspicion. They don't speak to me.
Skin color and expensive condos are the dividing line.

That tender spot that breathes inside has grown thick with scars.
It used to be I didn't feel lonely walking down my own
neighborhood.

On the Northwest Corner Of the 3200 Block Of West Thomas Street, Chicago

In the early evening
there is a quiet hurrying
I walk through my garden
to my garage

in the back alley
four children
five years my best friends
are missing,
they are not there to greet me
in the usual happy
after school way.

Strewn by my garbage cans
a ragged stuffed bear
nose in the mud
broken plastic cars
a little doll house with
a missing door;

ropes, tape, bent cartons
overflowing with family things
littered on the pavement.

You are moving suddenly
I remark to my neighbor
she stops her task for a moment;

a nervous smile
a mirror of her children's faces
she responds in Spanish—

He grabbed my littlest boy
by the neck, shook him hard
made a red mark, called him a spic;
the kids are afraid to play outside
all because

he's the new landlord
likes his tenants blonde
blue-eyed
childless, quiet
with office jobs
likes them with dogs
or a cat, but not with children.

All I have are my children,
two part-time jobs, and
a little time in the evening to rest

he says my cooking
stinks up his apartment
tells me *this isn't the projects*
yelled, *keep those niggers inside*

out of the way

threatened to call the police
if I'm not gone by tomorrow.

I will miss your tomatoes.

I shake my head—
one final embrace goodbye

continued…

*I will miss the smile in your
children's eyes.*

I think
this man has nails in his eyes
his tongue is a rope
his lips a noose

a fist rises up inside me
it is razor sharp
I want to smash his words
into pieces
I bite my anger back,

but that's all I do.

Lucky Find

Evicted neighbors
from the rear apartment
abandon a mattress
full size
two urine spots;

dragged by boys
seizing their luck
from the alley
to an empty lot

a kick-the-can game
is postponed—

lacking picnics
parks
swimming pools
strong arms, thin legs
catapult to the top of the world

spirits fly high
into the sky
bodies somersaulting
imagining a trampoline
a circus
cheering crowds

gym shoes slip-slide down
on broken glass
sharp stones
candy wrappers
a buried needle or two;

continued…

in the valley of a hot summer
nothing is easy in a
less than perfect world

their childhood is a taut rope
loosened by dipping into
some kind of softness even if
gravel burrows into their skin—

refusing to listen to the voice
of the night
they press their longings
into their hands
the outline of their flying figures
still jumping on the mattress
battered
dusty
in the early moon.

Roses

Clouds of them
all around the backyard
a hurricane of them

even between those places
nothing should grow
my mother plants another womb of roses.

Once we moved to a shady street
curtained in sadness she pointed
to the indifferent soil

Nada puede crecer aqui.

She planted tomatoes, peppers, cilantro;
in sympathy some grew small—
but never the roses.

Unexpectedly she came to live
with me
the first morning

her eyes were a young child's
hands folding roses into the ground while
inside my own petals were soft.

Early Morning Ritual

Coffee, dark, one cup at 5 A.M.
I wake to stare out the window
the mouth of the sky yawns—
born into light again
a small world without words

crowns the city in gray
then travels over us in blue.

Whatever my dreams
the night before
I can remember
only the faces of
suffering people
smeared on last
night's evening news.
The neighbor's dog whimpers.

I hold my cat close—

I wonder if my neighbors can
see me the way I see them;

a small sad bird rests on a wire
crossing the street a woman
hurries to her car
nearby a horn spits its noise
now an ambulance, a fire truck,
suddenly silence again.

I wish the best for all of them
I do.

Later,

children laughing on their way
to somewhere wave at me
they speak a language of happiness
I never knew.

Behind me books, oracles of my life
pencils in a cracked ceramic cup
point to me waiting

chores sprout like hearty phlox

dirty socks, wrinkled shirts
that should be in the washer wait
nothing needs to be done
this moment
I do not want a world of work today.

A cloud passes over the window
without blinking

I wish for more time.

Body Of Odd Thoughts

Waiting

From far
a voice,
perhaps a woman
praying;
the wind passes
touches my ear
then it is quiet.

A sleeping child
is ready to rise,
run
laugh
fall
somewhere.

In dim light
I wait for something
faint to stir

before it is
too late.

An Anaphora About Preferences

In honor of Waliska Zymborska

I prefer the morning sun to the sleepy-eyed evening horizon.
I prefer the whole awful truth to easy white lies.
I prefer one cup of coffee in the morning and one cup of tea
before I go to bed.
I prefer silence to too many voices talking at once.

I prefer books over movies and movies over T.V.
I prefer teachers who make mistakes and admit to them.
I prefer the laughter of children to the opera.
I prefer small incidents of poetic justice over one great
life lesson.

I prefer hot showers and sun dried towels.
I prefer to learn quickly from my stupidities.
I prefer serious questions I can't answer
to silly ones I can.
I prefer dubious endings to stories rather
than happy ones.
I prefer peace and peace of mind.

I prefer eating at home.
I prefer wine, red of course, at room temperature.
I prefer long hair that slaps my face on a windy day.
I prefer walking than waiting for a bus.
I prefer to believe in UFO's, ghosts, and that there
are no such things as coincidences.

I prefer to stand my ground.
I prefer to forgive.
I prefer to confess.
I prefer not to know some things—
some stories are too hard to bare.
I prefer the moon to the sun,
water to sand, and fire to wind

I prefer to love conditionally.
I prefer to take the risk.

Innocence

Feet floating over weeds
small stones, broken glass
in the abandoned lot

a young girl with dandelions
in her hands
plucked from the edge
of a fence crowned
with barb wire
thinks they are beautiful

their brown milky sap
stains her hands.

Flowers
she laughs—

as she hands them to her mother.

Answered Prayer

Breaking through the roof
past the ceiling of the trees
swinging from the vines of time

up
past the clouds' smoky faces

beyond the moon, stars, even comets
a child's prayer

long forgotten by the woman she has become
like a runaway kite

returns
as the cat
she always wanted.

Ode To Directions

I.
We're told we all need direction. We
spend a lifetime looking for them or
taking them, not realizing that sometimes
we reach our destination without direction.

II.
Written on a piece of paper, napkin, or
matchbook I misplace desperately needed
directions. A week later, I fold a piece
of masticated gum into that loose piece of
paper that had directions. I toss it out
the car window.

III.
Someone at the end of the street looks
confused. You know they are lost, but you
keep walking because you don't have time
to give directions. Or you just don't want to.
Let them figure it out for themselves, you
think. No one ever helped you with directions.
Plus, you might get mugged.

IV.
Birds, bees, and ants have an internal compass
that gives them directions. They fly over hills,
crawl under porches, and are able to find food. How come
we don't follow our own internal directions?
Maybe we wouldn't be so lost.

V.
Teachers are always giving directions. They get angry when students don't follow directions. Then they direct oppositional students to the principal's office where they get strict directions to go to the detention room.

VI.
Directions are painted onto stop signs. They are color-coded: yellow means yield and red means stop. Drivers enjoy disregarding those directions until a traffic cop directs them to pull over and gives them a ticket with directions on where to send the fine.

VII.
Teenagers don't like taking directions. They often end up in a lonely or dangerous place without directions. Later, most regret not taking directions. Some don't.

VIII.
Packaged foods have directions printed on the back or side of the box. The directions direct us on what to add, how to mix, and how long something must be cooked. Some directions are written in other languages or in pictures.

IX.
Sometimes there are too many direction. Sitting still in a place is a direction in itself.

continued…

X.
There are people who don't know where
they are going, but think they have direction.
These are some of the most dangerous people
in the world, especially when they want you
to take their direction.

XI.
When a middle-aged woman loses direction
she makes it an adventure. She rents her
house, lends her car to her daughter, and buys
a plane ticket to no where in particular to find
her new direction. She finds out what she
always wanted is the direction of home.

XII.
Stars give directions. They give the best kind.
In the mornings the sun directions your gaze
to the east. At night the sun directs your gaze
to the west. A falling star directs you to make
a wish that usually comes true. The Big Dipper
and all the constellations direct you to remember
everything always falls into place. Their
direction will never make you lose your way.

XIII.
This poem has traveled to a special location.
I have given you directions to my specific points.
We have reached our destination-the direction
is the end of this poem.

Would You Still Invite Frida Khalo To Dinner?

She was a
communist-loving
Stalin-supporting
anti-status quo revolutionary
bisexual swinger.
A rice and beans dish.

A narcissist
proletariat-backing
Marxist-socialist corroborating
pot smoking
border crossing
manic depressive
brown-skinned
Mexican-Jewish
lesbian.
Kosher when she wanted to be.

She was a hater of
los cabrones
disabled *pata de palo*
a lapsed Catholic
atheist and pantheist
cigar-smoking
subversive
cardajadas bell-laughing woman.
Meaty, seasoned, hot.

continued…

Audacious siempre.
Prejudice defying
misunderstood
defensive and arrogant
obsessive
medical student dropout.
Symbol chasing idealist.
An Olmec, Axtec, and Toltec,
all wrapped up into one enchilada.

An intellectual existentialist
questioning everything.
Independent
erotic personification
of a woman.
Never useless.
Never invisible.

Dare you?

All About Bull

I.
The bull emerges from the darkness
that invaded my dream
one night; in this dream I was a young
boy. I pierced the bull's heart with a
can opener after I figured it would
kill me if I didn't kill it first.
I woke up feeling relieved.

II.
Holding hands with my mother
she leads me up the aisle in
the Spanish theater that shows
Cantiflas movies from Mexico with
bull-fight updates from Spain.
I hold my bag of buttered popcorn close—
the kind that doesn't wait to
melt in your mouth, the kind that
melts in your nose. The bull's
nostrils flare on the screen. He
seems to want some popcorn, too.

III.
Driving north away from Chicago
the countryside is littered with cows,
but I see only one lonely bull. Is
he lonely?

IV.
On the streets of Pamplona
bulls charge men dressed in white
who purposely run in front of the bulls.
Some men get gashed. Some even die
Why do they do it? I must redefine
the meaning of "fun."

continued...

V.
If you stare into the eyes of a bull
you can see yourself in his. Who
are you when you peer so deeply into
his eyes? The bull knows who you
really are.

VI.
The bull's picture is on a beer
bottle. Who drew that picture?
Did they get permission from the
bull? Would the bull approve?
Is someone paying royalty fees to
the bull for the creative inspiration
we get from him?

VII.
When we look at a full moon
on those hot summer nights,
when we tire of reruns on T.V.
and we feel compelled to look
into the night sky…
why do we say we see a man on
the moon instead of a bull on the moon?

VIII.
Who is the bull's mother?
What is the feminine of bull?

IX.
Does the word bully derived
from the root word *bull*?
What about the words
*bulwark, bullet, bullhorn, bullish,
bull-headed*, and *bulletin*?

X.
I want to make bull
mean *love, hope, peace,* and *believe,*
So next time I say, "I
love bull" it will mean I love you.
"I have bull" will mean I have hope.
"Bull on earth" will mean peace on
earth, and "I bull in you" will mean
I believe in you…you know what I mean.

This is all about my love of bull.

About the Author

Yolanda Nieves, a Chicago born poetand playwright, is the recipient of various research and writing awards. Author of *Dove over Clouds* (Plainview Press, 2007) and the writer and director of the acclaimed play, "The Brown Girls' Chronicles," Ms. Nieves currently teaches developmental reading and writing to inner-city students.

www.ingramcontent.com/pod-product-compliance
Lightning Source LLC
Chambersburg PA
CBHW052100070526
44584CB00017B/2275